D0116735

MVFOL

WORLD RELIGIONS

FACTS ABOUT

HINDUISM

Alison Cooper

rosen publishing's
rosen central

New York

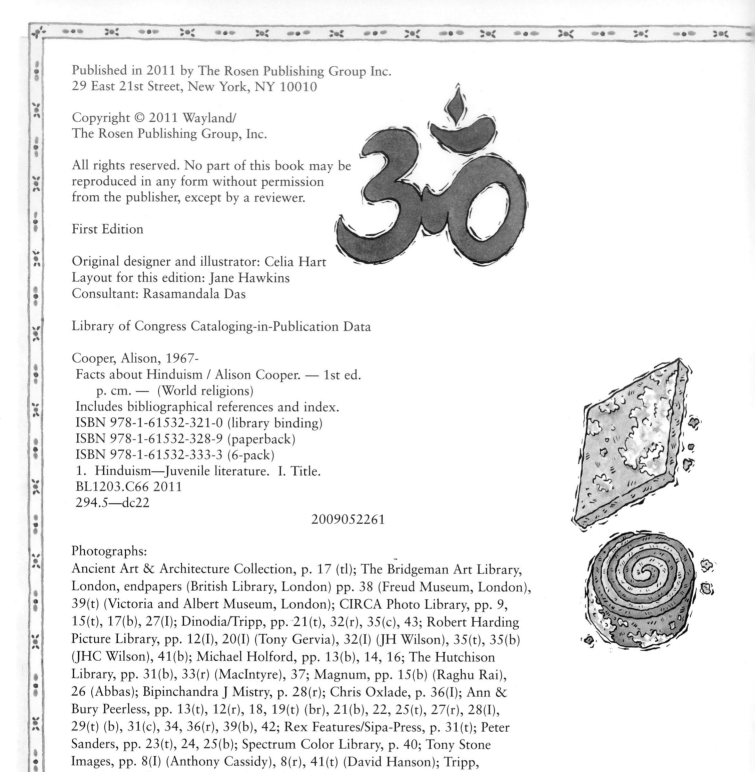

Published in 2011 by The Rosen Publishing Group Inc.
29 East 21st Street, New York, NY 10010

First Edition

Original designer and illustrator: Celia Hart
Layout for this edition: Jane Hawkins
Consultant: Rasamandala Das

Library of Congress Cataloging-in-Publication Data

Cooper, Alison, 1967-
  Facts about Hinduism / Alison Cooper. — 1st ed.
      p. cm. — (World religions)
  Includes bibliographical references and index.
  ISBN 978-1-61532-321-0 (library binding)
  ISBN 978-1-61532-328-9 (paperback)
  ISBN 978-1-61532-333-3 (6-pack)
  1. Hinduism—Juvenile literature. I. Title.
  BL1203.C66 2011
  294.5—dc22

                                    2009052261

Photographs:
Ancient Art & Architecture Collection, p. 17 (tl); The Bridgeman Art Library,
London, endpapers (British Library, London) pp. 38 (Freud Museum, London),
39(t) (Victoria and Albert Museum, London); CIRCA Photo Library, pp. 9,
15(t), 17(b), 27(I); Dinodia/Tripp, pp. 21(t), 32(r), 35(c), 43; Robert Harding
Picture Library, pp. 12(I), 20(I) (Tony Gervia), 32(I) (JH Wilson), 35(t), 35(b)
(JHC Wilson), 41(b); Michael Holford, pp. 13(b), 14, 16; The Hutchison
Library, pp. 31(b), 33(r) (MacIntyre), 37; Magnum, pp. 15(b) (Raghu Rai),
26 (Abbas); Bipinchandra J Mistry, p. 28(r); Chris Oxlade, p. 36(I); Ann &
Bury Peerless, pp. 13(t), 12(r), 18, 19(t) (br), 21(b), 22, 25(t), 27(r), 28(I),
29(t) (b), 31(c), 34, 36(r), 39(b), 42; Rex Features/Sipa-Press, p. 31(t); Peter
Sanders, pp. 23(t), 24, 25(b); Spectrum Color Library, p. 40; Tony Stone
Images, pp. 8(I) (Anthony Cassidy), 8(r), 41(t) (David Hanson); Tripp,
pp. 20(r) (Helene Rogers), 23(b) (Helene Rogers), 30 (W Jacobs), 33 (I)
(Helene Rogers).

Endpapers: This painting shows a scene from the
Ramayana, in which Rama and Sita are living in
exile in the forest.

Manufactured in China
CPSIA Compliance Information: Batch #W119230PK: For Further Information
contact Rosen Publishing, New York, New York at 1-800-237-9932

CONTENTS

Who Are the Hindus?   8

Timeline   10

How Did Hinduism Begin?   12

What Do Hindus Believe?   14

Which Are the Main Hindu Deities?   16

Do Hindus Worship Other Deities?   18

How Do Hindu Families Live?   20

Where Do Hindus Worship?   22

How Do Hindus Worship?   24

Who Are Hindu Holy Men?   26

Which Are the Hindus' Sacred Books?   28

Which Are the Hindus' Sacred Places?   30

What Are the Main Hindu Festivals?   32

What Are the Most Important Times in a Hindu's Life?   34

What Is Traditional Hindu Medicine?   36

What Is Hindu Art Like?   38

Do Hindus Like Music and Dance?   40

Do Hindus Like Stories?   42

Glossary and Further Reading   44

Index and Web Sites   45

WHO ARE THE HINDUS?

Hindus are followers of a religion called Hinduism. Hinduism began in India thousands of years ago and it

is one of the oldest religions in the world. Hindus themselves call their religion *sanatana dharma,* which means "eternal law" or "eternal teaching." Although most Hindus live in India, many have moved to other countries, such as the United States and the United Kingdom. There are also some Hindus who are not from Indian families.

◀ **Holy Man**

This holy man is a sannyasi (monk) who has left home in search of God. Holy men are often called sadhus. They give up all their possessions and wander from place to place praying and meditating.

▲ **Hindu Temple**

This Hindu temple is in Bali, Indonesia, showing how Hinduism has spread far from India.

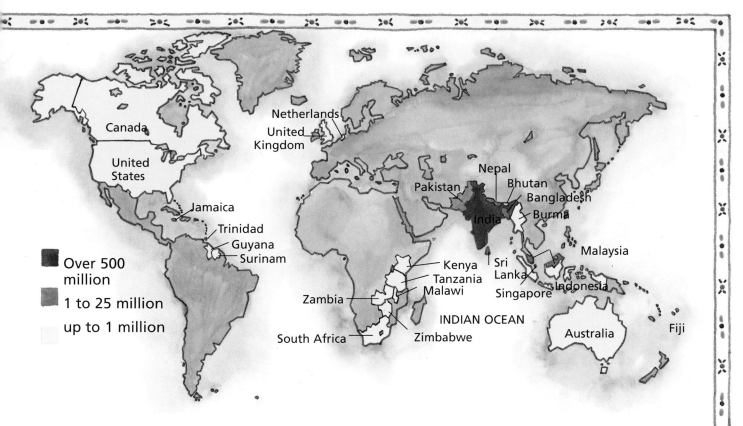

The Hindu World

There are about 700 million Hindus worldwide. Most live in India and its nearby countries. Traders spread Hinduism to parts of Southeast Asia 1,000 years ago. Indians who went to Africa and the Caribbean in the nineteenth century took their religion with them. In the twentieth century, many Hindus settled in the UK, Canada, and the U.S.A.

Map labels: Canada, Netherlands, United Kingdom, United States, Nepal, Pakistan, Bhutan, Bangladesh, India, Burma, Jamaica, Trinidad, Guyana, Surinam, Kenya, Sri Lanka, Malaysia, Tanzania, Malawi, Zambia, Singapore, Indonesia, South Africa, Zimbabwe, INDIAN OCEAN, Australia, Fiji

Key:
- Over 500 million
- 1 to 25 million
- up to 1 million

AN ANCIENT NAME

The word Hindu was used by the ancient Persians (who lived in the area of modern-day Iran) over 2,000 years ago. They used the name to describe the people who lived east of the River Indus, in what is now Pakistan.

▲ Hindu Worshipers

These worshipers are in a temple in the UK. Hindus came to the UK in the 1950s from countries such as India and Sri Lanka. Many more came from East Africa in the late 1960s and early 1970s. Today, many young Hindus in the UK are British-born.

TIMELINE

THE DEVELOPMENT OF HINDUISM

C.E. = Common Era—this refers to the same time period as A.D. (Anno Domini, "in the year of our Lord") traditionally used in the Christian world
B.C.E. = Before the Common Era

C. 3000 B.C.E. Krishna appeared and spoke to Bhagavad Gita, according to Hindu texts.	C. 2500 B.C.E. The great cities of the Indus valley are at the height of their power.	C. 1500 B.C.E. The Aryan people begin to invade India, according to scholars. Hinduism begins to develop.	C. 1500–1000 B.C.E. The *Vedas* are used by priests. The system of 4 varnas and 4 ashrams develops.	C. 800 B.C.E. The *Upanishads* are composed.	C. 500 B.C.E. The Buddha spreads his teaching and lays the foundations for Buddhism

◀ Seal used by Indus valley peoples

Buddha ▶

1828 C.E. The Brahmo Samaj (Society of God) is founded, seeking to reform Hinduism.	1757 C.E. India starts to come under British power and becomes part of the British Empire in 1858.	1600s–1700s C.E. Many Europeans arrive in India, mainly to trade.	1632 C.E. Shah Jehan builds the Taj Mahal in Agra as a memorial to his wife.	1570s C.E. The saint Tulsi Das writes the *Ram Charit Manas*, a poem based on the *Ramayana*.	1556–1605 C.E. The Mogul emperor, Akbar the Great, is emperor of India.
1857 C.E. First Indian war of independence against the British.	Taj Mahal			The flag of India ▶	
1869 C.E. Birth of Mahatma Gandhi, a great leader in India's struggle for independence.	1875 C.E. The Arya Samaj, another Hindu reform movement, is formed.	1876 C.E. Queen Victoria takes the title Empress of India.	1897 C.E. The Ramakrishna Mission is established in Calcutta.	1910 C.E. Sri Aurobindo starts a religious center in Pondicherry, India.	1947 C.E. India gains independenc but is split into Hindu India and Muslim Pakistan.

New Countries

Great Britain ruled India from the late eighteenth century until 1947. Most Indians were Hindus but there were also a large number of Muslims. When India gained independence, the country's Muslims called for a separate nation to be set up where they would be free to rule themselves. Their demand was granted. The western state of Punjab and the eastern state of Bengal became West and East Pakistan. East Pakistan became Bangladesh in 1971. The partition of India led to terrible violence between Hindus and Muslims and many people were forced to leave their homes.

400 B.C.E.–400 C.E. Large parts of the *Ramayana* and *Mahabharata* are composed.	320–550 C.E. The Gupta kings rule India—a "golden age" for Hinduism.	C. 700–800 C.E. The Hindu Mataram kingdom is established in Java, Indonesia.	C. 800 C.E. The great philosopher Shankara teaches about the *Upanishads*.
			C. 900 C.E. The Chola kings rule south India. Many beautiful temples are built.

▲ Coin of the Gupta kings

1526 C.E. The Muslim Mogul Empire is founded in India.	1469 C.E. The birth of Guru Nanak, founder of the Sikh religion. Bhakti saints popular at this time.	1206–1555 C.E. Muslims are powerful in the north, but a Hindu kingdom thrives in south India.	C. 1050 C.E. Ramanuja, a Hindu philosopher, teaches devotion to a personal God, in south India.

◀ Mahatma Gandhi

Swastika ▶

1948 C.E. Mahatma Gandhi is assassinated.	1950s–1960s C.E. Many Hindus leave India to live in the UK, Canada, and the United States.	1960s–1970s C.E. Many Hindus arrive in the UK, especially from East Africa, and establish the first temples.

Sign of Luck ▲

In the twentieth century, a version of the swastika became the symbol of the German Nazi Party. It became associated with evil. For Hindus, however, it is an ancient symbol of luck and good fortune.

HOW DID HINDUISM BEGIN?

Many Hindus believe that religion is forever and that their own tradition goes back thousands, even millions of years. Scholars say that Hinduism began over 4,000 years ago. Clay figures found in the ruins of Indus valley cities look similar to the deities (representations of God) worshiped by Hindus today.

The religion of the Indus valley people combined with the beliefs of people called the Aryans. The Aryans arrived in India from the northwest in around 1500 B.C.E. They worshiped many deities mostly linked to the natural world.

Two Great Cities ▼

Archaeologists began excavating the Indus valley cities of Harappa and Mohenjo Daro in the 1920s. Each had a hilltop fort (see below), used as a temple and government building. Hundreds of stone seals have been found among the ruins. Many show sacred animals, such as bulls or elephants, and merchants used them to mark their goods.

Seal showing a bull

▲ King or Priest?

This carved stone head was found at Mohenjo Daro. It could be the head of a king, or a priest with his eyes closed in meditation.

RITUALS AND SACRIFICES

The Aryans believed that health and good harvests were dependent on the good will of God and the various deities. Their priests would throw offerings of grains, spices, butter, and milk into the sacred fire. Goats and horses were sometimes sacrificed, too. As the priests performed the sacrifices, they sang hymns and chanted mantras (sacred spells). The Aryans believed that the deities could accept offerings through the flames of a fire.

Agni ▲

The carving above shows Agni, the god of fire and sacrifice. He was one of the most important Aryan deities.

◄ Indra

Indra was the most popular Aryan god, famous for his bravery and strength. He was the god of war and also of storms and thunder. His weapon was the thunderbolt. In this picture, he is riding his white battle elephant.

WHAT DO HINDUS BELIEVE?

Most Hindus share the same basic beliefs, even though they do not all worship in the same way. One important teaching is reincarnation. This

means that when you die, your soul is reborn in the body of another human or animal. You can be reborn many times. Hindus hope that by leading a good life they will break free of the cycle of death and rebirth and achieve salvation, or moksha.

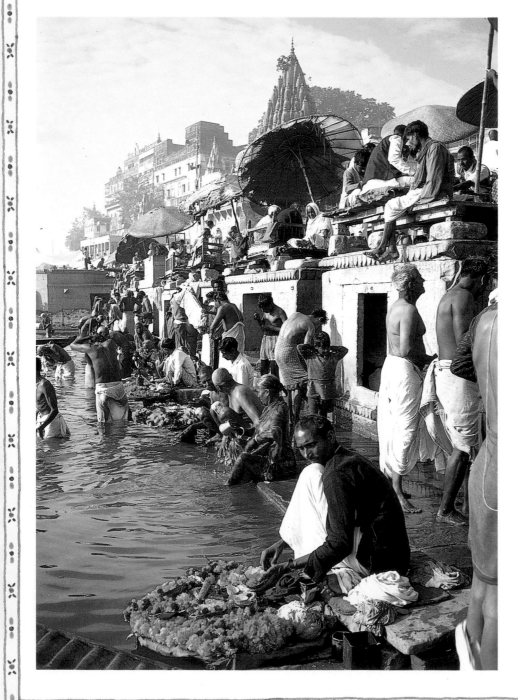

◀ **Sacred River**
These Hindus are bathing in the River Ganges in India. They believe that the water of the Ganges is holy. By bathing in it they wash away their sins and come closer to achieving moksha.

▲ **Sacred Sound**
This symbol is the sound "Om." Hindus recite this sound during meditation and at the beginning of prayers and mantras.

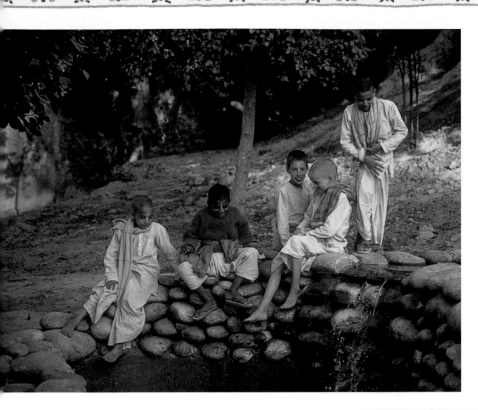

◀ Monastery Schools

These boys are being educated at an ashram. An ashram is a place or community for spiritual development. The boys are taught by priests and religious teachers called gurus. The pupils treat their gurus with great respect. Adult Hindus sometimes spend time at an ashram to seek spiritual guidance.

A Way of Life ▶

Hindus try to follow a sacred code of behavior called dharma. This means serving God and doing their duty to family, friends, and society. Religion affects everything in their daily life, from working honestly to the food they eat, which is often vegetarian.

 PATHS TO FOLLOW

There are four paths Hindus can follow to reach moksha.

- The Path of Devotion—prayer, worship, and devotion to God.
- The Path of Knowledge—study and learning, with a guru's guidance.
- The Path of Right Action—acting without any thought of reward for yourself.
- The Path of Yoga—yoga and meditation.

WHICH ARE THE MAIN HINDU DEITIES?

The deities of Hinduism represent different characteristics of Brahman, the supreme soul or spirit. Brahman is all around, in everything, all the time. The three main deities are Brahma the creator, Vishnu the protector, and Shiva the destroyer.

A Hindu may worship more than one deity, though they often have a favorite or one they consider to be the supreme deity (God). Often, a family has worshiped certain deities for several generations.

◀ Brahma

This is a statue of Brahma, the creator of the universe and the god of wisdom. The sacred statue has four faces (although only three can be seen in this photograph). This shows that Brahma looks over the whole world—north, south, east, and west. He has four arms, too, in which he holds the sacred books, the prayer beads, and the water pot of a holy man. Brahma, although important as the creator, is only worshiped in one place in India.

Shiva ▼

Shiva, the destroyer of the world, is often shown dancing. The dance represents the energy flowing through the world, which causes day and night, the changing seasons, death and rebirth.

Dancing Shiva

Vishnu ▲

The painting above shows Vishnu, the protector of the universe, with his wife, Lakshmi. She is the goddess of wealth and good fortune. Vishnu has come to earth nine times, in nine different forms, or avatars, to save the world. These include Lord Rama, Lord Krishna, and Buddha. The tenth avatar of Vishnu is Kalki, the rider on the white horse, who is yet to come.

RIDING ANIMALS

The various deities ride on different animals. For example, Brahma rides on a swan, Vishnu rides on a giant eagle (above), and Shiva rides on a white bull named Nandi (right).

DO HINDUS WORSHIP OTHER DEITIES?

There are thousands of Hindu deities. Some are worshiped all over India, others are honored in just one or two villages. The most worshiped are Vishnu, Shiva, and the goddess Parvati.

Rama and Krishna are two of the avatars (forms) of Vishnu. Parvati is the wife of Shiva. Like many Hindu deities, she has other names, representing her different aspects. When she is worshiped as Kali or Durga, she is awesome and terrifying. She represents the destruction of evil and the protection of good.

◀ Rama and Sita

The picture on the left shows Rama, his wife Sita, and his faithful friend, Hanuman, the monkey god. The story of Rama and Sita is told in the great poem, the *Ramayana* (see pages 42–43). Rama is worshiped as an ideal human being—a great hero, a devoted husband, and a just king.

SUN AND MOON

Surya, the sun god, rides across the sky each morning in his golden chariot. His wife, Ushas, is goddess of the dawn.

Surya

The silver chariot of Chandra, the moon god, crosses the sky as darkness falls.

Chandra

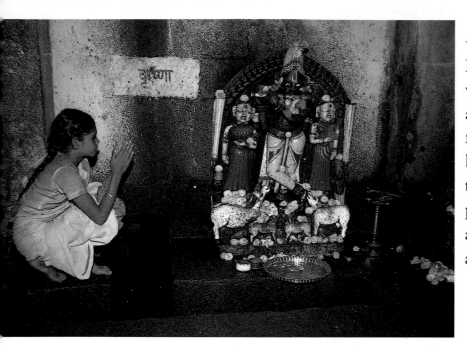

◀ Krishna

Krishna is usually shown with dark blue or black skin and carrying or playing a flute. He is often surrounded by cows and milkmaids, too. Krishna is famous for playing tricks on his friends and is the hero of many adventures.

Durga ▶

Durga is the warlike form of the goddess Parvati. In this picture, she is riding on a fierce tiger and holding a different weapon in each of her ten hands.

Ganesh ▲

Ganesh is the son of Shiva and Parvati. Hindus pray to him before they begin anything new because he is the god who removes obstacles.

HOW DO HINDU FAMILIES LIVE?

It is traditional for Hindus to share their home with their parents, grandparents, uncles, aunts, and cousins. Large family groups such as this are known as joint or extended families. Children learn about their religion from their parents and grandparents. They are taught to respect the older members of their family.

◀ Family Names
Hindus rarely call one another by their first names. They use special titles that describe how they are related. For instance, you would call your father's younger brother *chachaji* and his wife *chachiji*. The man in the center of the photograph on the left has just married the girl in the red sari. She will soon be getting to know his relatives because she will live in their family home.

Caste System ▶
Hindus divided society into four groups called varnas. Traditionally, this was based on the jobs people did. The highest varna is the priests. Next come the warriors and nobles, and after them the merchants. Below them are the laborers, such as the potters in this photograph. The present system, based on the community you are born in, is called the caste system.

Sweets

Vegetarian Food ▲

Many Hindus are vegetarians because they think it is wrong to kill animals to eat. A typical meal might include a spicy vegetable dish, rice, dhal, and flatbread. With their meal people drink water, sweet tea, or a yogurt drink called lassi.

◀Indian Sweets ▲

Many Hindus love sweets and they are often given as gifts at weddings and festivals. Milk, cheese, nuts, coconut, and sugar are popular ingredients.

Sacred Cows ▲

Hindus believe that the cow is very special because she is a mother that produces milk, a precious source of food. Wherever you go in India, you will see cows wandering freely, even in the towns.

NAMES

Many Hindu children are named after deities, or have names that are linked to their religion.

Boys
Rajendra—Lord Indra
Mahesh—a name of Shiva

Girls
Devi—goddess
Vandana—worshiper

WHERE DO HINDUS WORSHIP?

For many Hindus, there are no set rules about where they should worship, or when. Some Hindus set up a shrine in a room at home and worship there. They also worship in buildings called temples, or *mandirs*. Some people visit the temple every day. Others only go there at special times, such as festivals. Hindu temples are often noisy, lively places, filled with the sound of praying, chanting, and singing.

◄ Temples

This is the entrance gateway of a temple in southern India. It is decorated with carvings of the deity. People think of the temple as the earthly home of God. This temple is dedicated to Shiva.

Temple Bell ▲

As worshipers enter the temple, they ring the bell to announce their arrival.

Street Shrines ▶

On many street corners, there are small shrines like this one, where Hindus can stop to worship on their way to work or school. They might leave an offering of flowers or sweets for the deity. This shrine is dedicated to Shiva. You can see the white bull, Nandi, in the bottom left corner.

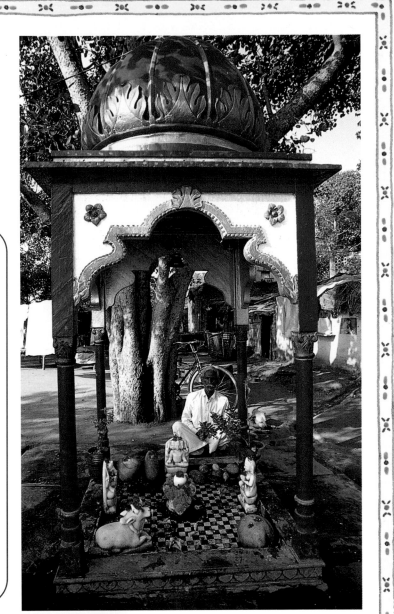

MORE TEMPLES

The only temple in India dedicated to Brahma is in Pushkar, in western India. In southern India, at Mahabalipuram, there is a group of very beautiful stone temples. They are 1,400 years old.
The town is still famous for the skill of its sculptors.

Temples at Mahabalipuram

◀ Worship at Home

The photograph on the left shows a shrine in a Hindu home. It is dedicated to Saraswati, the goddess of art and music and the wife of Brahma. The brass pots on the floor contain leaves, flowers, and candies, which the family will offer to the goddess for her blessing.

HOW DO HINDUS WORSHIP?

There is no set time when Hindus should visit the temple—but mornings and evenings are most important. Before they enter the building, they take off their shoes. Women often cover their heads, to show respect. Hindus go to the temple to take darshan of the deity as well as for group worship. Darshan means a "seeing" of the image or statue in the inner sanctum that shows the presence of the deity.

▲ The Inner Sanctum

A priest sits near the image of the deity in the inner sanctum, the holiest part of the temple. Only the priest is allowed to get so close to the sacred image.

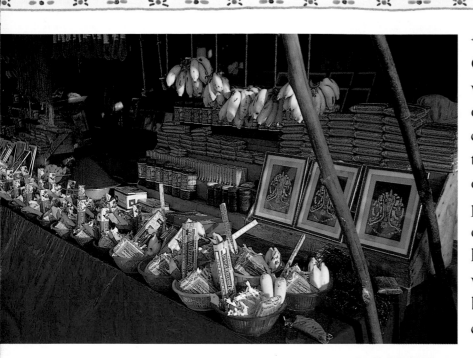

◄ Temple Offerings

Outside the temple, worshipers can buy offerings of flowers, fruit, incense, and colored powder at stalls like this one. They give their offerings to the priest and he presents them to the temple deity to be blessed. Then he hands them back to the worshiper, to carry the deity's blessing back to them. This ceremony is part of puja.

In the Temple ►

These worshipers are waiting for a darshana (sight) of the god Hanuman. They are holding offerings of flower garlands and small lamps. As part of their worship, they circle the shrine. They always walk in a clockwise direction to keep their right sides facing toward the god and the inner sanctum.

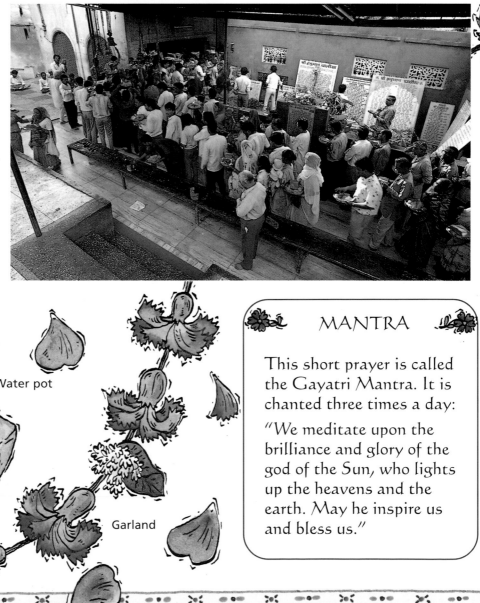

Water pot

Garland

MANTRA

This short prayer is called the Gayatri Mantra. It is chanted three times a day:

"We meditate upon the brilliance and glory of the god of the Sun, who lights up the heavens and the earth. May he inspire us and bless us."

WHO ARE HINDU HOLY MEN?

Hindu holy men include priests, gurus, and sannyasi. A sannyasi is a person who has given up his home, family, and possessions to lead a life of prayer and meditation. Some holy men wander from place to place and rely on local people to give them food and shelter. Others live on an ashram and learn from a guru, or teacher.

Holy Man ▶

This holy man, or sadhu, is a follower of Shiva. The cloth he is wearing around his waist is of a color called saffron, which is a holy color. He is meditating on the banks of the River Ganges. Many Hindus worship not only God but also holy men, especially gurus, and dedicate shrines to them.

 HOLY WORDS

These are some words spoken by famous Hindu holy men:

"I have nothing new to teach the world. Truth and nonviolence are as old as the hills."
Mahatma Gandhi

"A person who accepts a gift from the gods and does not repay it is a thief."
Sri Aurobindo

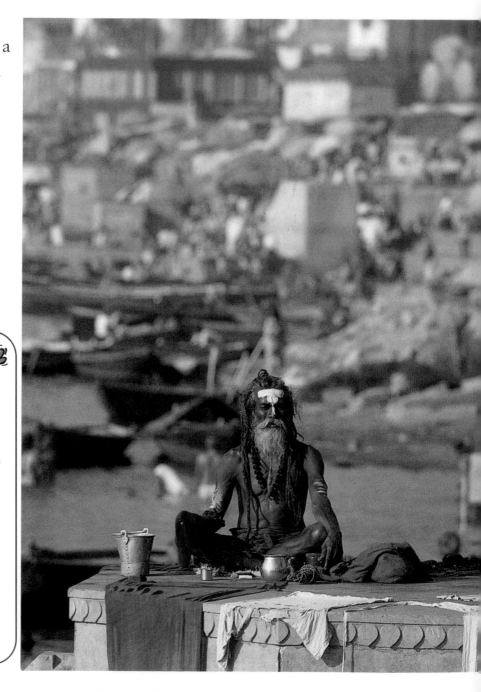

Ramakrishna ▼

A holy man named Ramakrishna taught that all religions were equal. He believed in Jesus Christ and in Muhammad, the founder of Islam, as well as in the Hindu gods. This temple belongs to the Ramakrishna Mission, which spread Ramakrishna's message.

Yoga and Meditation ▼

Many Hindus use yoga exercises and meditation. They train their bodies and minds to achieve moksha. Some people concentrate hard on a pattern to help them focus their minds. These patterns are called yantras.

iests ▲

very temple has its own priest *(pujari)*, who oks after the image of the temple deity and rforms the puja (ritual worship). Most indus have their own family priest, who mes to their home to perform important remonies.

Sacred conch shell

Prayer beads

Yantra

WHICH ARE THE HINDUS' SACRED BOOKS?

The *Veda* are the oldest of the Hindus' sacred books. They date from the time of the Aryans and are over 3,000 years old. Another important collection of teachings is the *Upanishads*. Hindus believe that a group of wise men heard the words of the *Upanishads* and the *Veda* directly from God.

The *Mahabharata* and the *Ramayana* are two long poems. These were also made up long ago and people learned them by heart. The words were passed down from one generation to another.

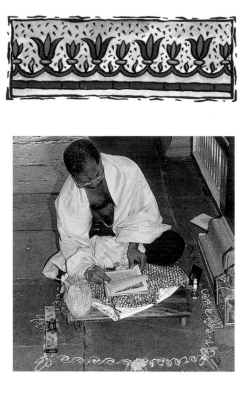

The Upanishads ▶

The photograph on the right shows words from the *Upanishads* carved on the wall of a temple in Varanasi, India. The *Upanishads* focus on the relationship between the atman (soul) and Brahman (the Supreme). These sacred teachings date from around 800 B.C.E.

श्रीलक्ष्मीनारायण

एक ही ईश्वर के अनेक नाम
स ब्रह्मा स शिवः सेन्द्रः सोऽक्षरः परमः स्वराट् ।
स एव विष्णुः स प्राणः स कालोऽग्निःस चन्द्रमाः ॥ (कैवल्य उप.१/८)
सर्वशक्तिमान् और समस्त जगत् का प्रकाशकवह परमात्मा ही ब्रह्मा (सृष्टि-कर्ता) है वही शिव रुद्र (विनाशक शक्ति) है, वही विष्णु (पालन करने वाली शक्ति) है वही इन्द्र है अविनाशी है वही सर्वव्यापक है, वही जगत् का जीवनाधार है वही काल है, अग्नि है, और चन्द्रमा है ।
He is one and only one God
THAT ALMIGHTY, ALLPERVADING GOD IS BRAHMA, THE CREATIVE FORM, VISHNU THE PROTECTIVE FORM AND SHIVA, THE DESTRUCTIVE FORM. HE IS INDRA; HE IS IMMORTAL; HE IS SELF-EXISTENT AND SELF-EFFULGENT. HE IS LIFE-FORM, HE IS TIME, HE IS FIRE AND HE IS MOON. (K. UPANISHAD 1/8)

SANSKRIT

Sanskrit is the ancient language of the Aryans. It is the language that was used when the *Veda* and the *Upanishads* were written down. Sanskrit is not much spoken now although it is still studied by priests. Hindi, the modern language of India, developed from it.

◀ Bhagavad Gita

The *Bhagavad Gita* is the most important and popular part of the *Mahabharata*. The *Mahabharata* tells the story of a war between two royal families, the Kauravas and the Pandavas, who are cousins. They both want to control the kingdom of Hastinapura, but the Pandavas are its rightful rulers.

The *Bhagavad Gita*, the "Song of the Lord," is set on the battlefield. The painting shows Arjuna, one of the Pandavas, in his chariot. Lord Krishna is his charioteer. Arjuna tells Krishna how sad he feels because he is about to fight his cousins. Krishna tells him to control his emotions and do his duty as a warrior. Acting selflessly is the way to achieve moksha. Arjuna follows Krishna's advice and eventually the Kaurava army is destroyed.

◀ The Ramayana

The *Ramayana* tells the story of Rama and Sita (you can read the story on pages 42–43). The poem was made up over 2,000 years ago, but the most famous version was written in the 1570s by Tulsi Das, who is shown in the picture on the left. It has also been made into a television series.

WHICH ARE THE HINDUS' SACRED PLACES?

Many sacred places are connected to events in the lives of various deities and the many Hindu saints. Some are famous for their beauty or because people have been miraculously healed there. Every year, millions of Hindus set off on journeys to visit sacred places. These journeys are called pilgrimages. People might go on a pilgrimage to ask God or specific deities to grant them a special request, or to give thanks to them. Sometimes, people walk for many days to reach a place of pilgrimage.

◀ Holy Places

This map shows some of the holiest places in India. Hindus believe they can pass beyond this world to obtain moksha at some of these sites.

Varanasi ▶

The city of Varanasi is the holiest place of pilgrimage. Hindu legends say that Shiva chose Varanasi as his home on earth. Most Hindus believe Varanasi is the best place to die and many go there to scatter the ashes of their dead relatives in the River Ganges. Pilgrims wash away their sins in its holy waters.

◀ Bathing Fairs

Every 12 years, a great fair is held at Allahabad. Over two million pilgrims come to bathe at the point where the River Ganges, the River Yamuna, and the mythical River Saraswati flow together. This type of fair is called a *kumbha mela*.

LEGEND OF THE GANGES

There was once a king who begged Shiva to let the magical River Ganges fall to earth. Shiva agreed to his request, but to make sure the earth would not shatter under the weight of the water, he caught the river in his hair. Then he let it flow down gently from the Himalayas.

Rameshwaram ▲

This is the Ramanathaswamy temple on the island of Rameshwaram in south India. Rama is said to have worshiped here after his battle with Ravana (see pages 42–43). It is an important place of pilgrimage.

Sacred Mountains ▶

The Himalayan mountains, which stretch across northern India, are the highest mountains in the world. Many of them are holy places. These pilgrims are making the difficult journey to Gangotri, the source of the River Ganges.

WHAT ARE THE MAIN HINDU FESTIVALS?

Hindus hold festivals to celebrate important events in the lives of their deities and saints. Festivals are also linked to the changing seasons and to harvest time. There are far too many festivals for everyone to celebrate all of them, but most Hindus celebrate Diwali, Holi, and Dussehra. For Hindus living outside India, festivals are an important way for children to learn about their religion and a time for families and friends to get together.

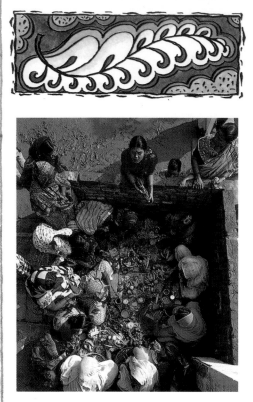

◄ Local Festivals

These women are preparing offerings. Local festivals celebrate the harvest or honor the village deities. Some festivals, such as the kite-flying festival in western India, are not religious— they are just lots of fun.

Kite

Diwali ►

Diwali is the Hindu festival of lights and it is celebrated in late October or early November. People light small oil lamps and place them by their doors and windows to guide Rama back home (see the story on pages 42–43). They enjoy firework displays and delicious food. They also give each other cards and presents.

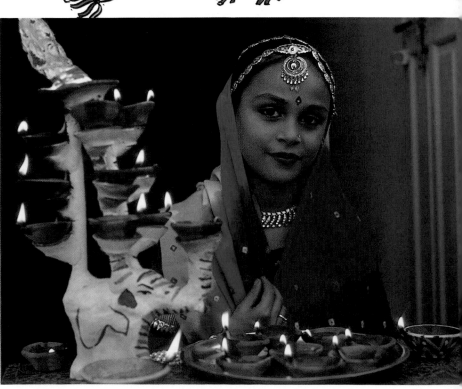

Dussehra ▶

The Dussehra festival is held in October. For most Hindus, it is a celebration of Rama's victory over the demon king, Ravana. Giant models of Ravana are used in a performance of the story.

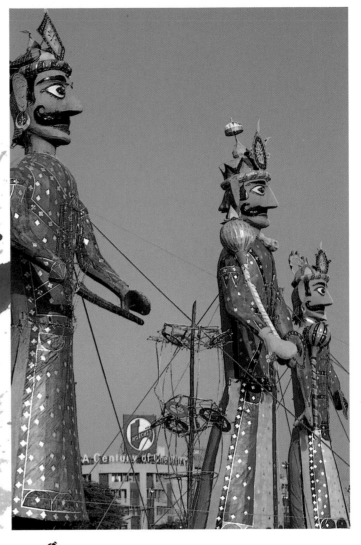

Holi ▲

Holi is the liveliest and messiest festival of the year. It is held in March to celebrate the coming of spring. People put on old clothes and pelt each other with colored water and powder. After a bath and change of clothes, they visit their relatives to wish them happy Holi.

Rakhi bracelets

Raksha Bandhan ▶

At Raksha Bandhan, brothers and sisters show their affection for each other. Girls tie bracelets called *rakhis* around their brothers' wrists. Boys give their sisters a gift.

HINDU CALENDAR

HINDU MONTH	
Chaitra	March–April
Vaisakha	April–May
Jyaishtha	May–June
Ashadha	June–July
Shravana	July–August
Bhadra	August–September
Ashvina	September–October
Karttika	October–November
Margashirsha	November–December
Pausha	December–January
Magha	January–February
Phalguna	February–March

WHAT ARE THE MOST IMPORTANT TIMES IN A HINDU'S LIFE?

Hindus mark important times in their lives with ceremonies called samskaras. These begin even before a baby is born, with prayers for it to be healthy and happy. Once the baby arrives, there are ceremonies to mark its birth, the first time it sees the sun, and its first haircut. Getting married is another important occasion marked with a samskara. The final ceremonies take place when a person dies and is cremated.

Horoscope ▶

The picture on the right is a horoscope for a baby boy. It shows the position of the stars and planets at the exact moment of the baby's birth. A priest draws up the horoscope and uses it to figure out what may happen to the baby in the future. This is done at the baby's naming ceremony, which usually takes place ten days after its birth.

Baby boy's horoscope

▼ Sacred Thread

Boys from the top three varnas—Brahmins, Kshatriyas, and Vaishyas—go through the sacred thread ceremony when they are about nine or ten years old. A priest loops a cotton thread over the boy's left shoulder and under his right arm. This marks the start of his adult life. He can now begin to study the holy books and take more responsibility within the family.

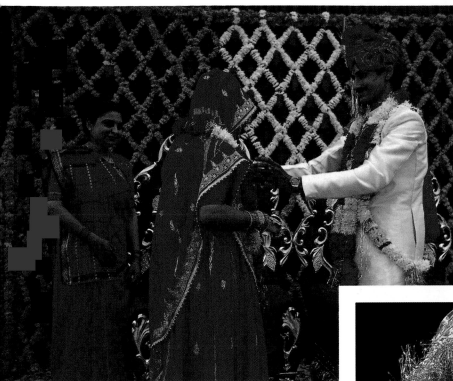

◄ A Hindu Wedding ▼

A Hindu wedding lasts
for several days and often
15 rituals are performed. In
the photograph on the left,
the bride and groom are
exchanging flower garlands.
The bride below is wearing
beautiful jewelry. The groom
will give her a special
necklace.

STAGES OF LIFE

A Hindu man's life is traditionally divided
into four stages:
Brahmachari—Life as a student
Grihastha—Married life
Vanaprastha—Retirement
Sannyas—Life as a wandering holy man

Death and Cremation ►

Hindus are almost always
cremated. The person's
eldest son or male relation
lights the fire while a priest
chants from the holy books.
Burning the body helps the
soul give up attachment to
the body and move onto
the next life. If possible,
people scatter the ashes of
their dead relative in the
River Ganges.

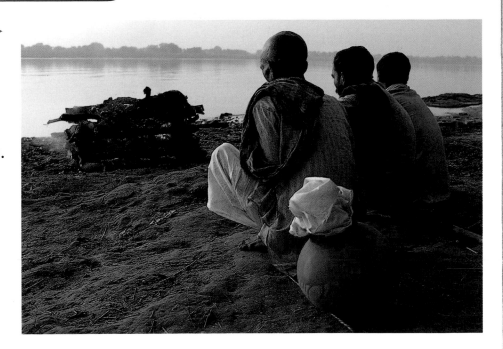

WHAT IS HINDU ART LIKE?

A lot of Hindu art is linked to religion. There are many sacred statues of the deities. Often, these are made for the inner sanctum of the temple or a family shrine. They are a symbol of God's presence on earth. Hindu artists also produce beautiful paintings and carvings that show scenes and stories from the sacred books. Many of the tools used by artists and sculptors have not changed in hundreds of years.

◄ Sacred Statue of Vishnu

This statue of Vishnu is carved from ivory. It shows him sitting on the coils of a serpent while he waits for Brahma to create the world. In his four arms, he holds the signs of his divinity and power: a conch shell, a lotus flower, a club, and a discus (spinning disk used as a weapon).

Symbol of Shiva ▼

The picture below shows a lingam, carved in stone or marble. It is a symbol of Shiva's presence and power. In temples dedicated to Shiva, there is often a lingam in the inner sanctum instead of a sacred statue of the god.

Shiva lingam

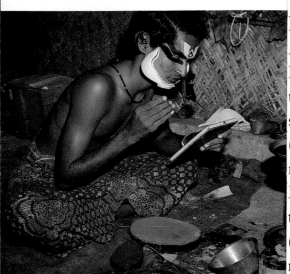

Hindu Painting ▶

Artists in Rajasthan, western India, painted this picture in the 1700s. It shows Vishnu surrounded by his ten avatars (see page 17). From left to right, they are: (top row) Matsysa the fish, Kurma the tortoise, Varaha the boar; (second row) Narasimha the man-lion, Vamana the dwarf; (third row) Parashurama the warrior, Rama; (bottom row) Krishna, the Buddha, and Kalki, the horseman.

Kathakali Dancers ▼

The masked dancers below are performing a Kathakali dance. This style of dancing is from southern India. All the dancers are men and they perform very dramatic dances based on the great Hindu poems.

A Modern Temple ▼

The temple below was built in Varanasi in 1964 in honor of the poet, Tulsi Das. In the 1570s, he produced a very famous version of the *Ramayana* called the *Ram Charit Manas*.

SYMBOLS USED IN ART

The swastika is an ancient sign of good fortune.

Om stands for perfection.

The lotus flower is a symbol of Vishnu.

The Sri symbol is a sign of wellbeing.

DO HI
Hindus love musi
Classical Hindu

▲ Classical Music

Indian classical music is ba
called ragas. Each raga has
as joy or sadness. The musi
(left to right) tablas (drums
and a sarangi (played with

MUSICAL I

The pictures above right sh
Tanpura—a stringed instru
Shahnai—a wind instrume
holes.
Rudra-vina—a stringed ins

DO HINDUS LIKE STORIES?

Hindus have enjoyed stories for thousands of years. Before the sacred books were written down, storytellers learned them by heart and went from village to village, telling tales of the deities and heroes, such as Rama and Krishna. Hindu children still read these stories in comic books and watch them on television. One of the best-loved tales is this story of Rama and Sita.

The Story of the Ramayana

Rama was the eldest son of the king of Ayodhya, a city in northern India. Rama was the rightful heir to the throne but his stepmother wanted her own son, Bharata, to be the king's heir. She persuaded the king to banish Rama from the kingdom for 14 years. Sadly, Rama left home with his wife, Sita, and his brother, Lakshman, and they went to live in the forest.

One day, while Rama and Lakshman were out hunting deer, Sita was kidnapped by Ravana, the demon king of Lanka. Rama and Lakshman looked for her everywhere, but she had vanished without trace. Eventually, Rama asked his friend Hanuman, the monkey god,

to help. Hanuman was the leader of a great army and had many magical powers.

After searching for a long time, Hanuman discovered that Ravana had taken Sita to Lanka, his island across the sea. With a giant leap he soared over the sea to the island and found Sita in the palace garden, surrounded by demon guards. But before Hanuman could get away to tell Rama, the guards caught him. Ravana tied him up with ropes and ordered the guards to set fire to his tail. Sita prayed to the gods to save Hanuman and they did. He escaped with only a singed tail.

Rama and Lakshman gathered a huge army, led by Hanuman and Jambhavan, the king of the bears. They built a bridge across the sea to Lanka and marched across it to do battle. Ravana sent his most terrifying demons to fight them and the battle raged all night. In the morning, Rama and Lakshman lay bleeding among the wounded.

Quickly, Hanuman realized what he must do. He dashed away to bring healing herbs from the top of a mountain and with them, saved his friends' lives. Now it was time for Rama to face the demon king himself.

Ravana ▲

The ten-headed demon king ruled the island that is now called Sri Lanka. He had been told that if he married Sita, he would become ruler of the world.

CAST LIST

King Dasharatha	Rama's father
Rama	An avatar of Vishnu, born on earth as a royal prince
Lakshman Shatrughna Bharata	Rama's brothers
Sita	Rama's wife
Ravana	King of Lanka
Indrajit	Ravana's son
Jambhavan	King of the bears
Hanuman The monkey warrior	

Ravana raced toward Rama in his war chariot. Calmly, Rama fitted a golden arrow to his golden bow and fired it at Ravana's heart. With a dreadful shriek, Ravana fell from his chariot and died.

At last, Rama and Sita were reunited. Together with Lakshman and Hanuman, they returned to Ayodhya. There, they were crowned king and queen and everyone rejoiced to see them.

••••

The story of Rama and Sita is acted out during the festival of Dussehra (see page 33).

▲ **Play Acting**
These children are dressed as Rama and Sita.

43